SUPER SCIENCE

I0895126

WEATHER

WRITTEN BY

Valerie Harvey

KidHaven PUBLISHING

Published in 2027 by
KidHaven Publishing, an Imprint of Greenhaven Publishing, LLC
2544 Clinton St., Buffalo, NY 14224

Written by: Valerie Harvey
Edited by: Nicola Chave
Designed by: Jasmine Pointer

Cataloging-in-Publication Data

Names: Harvey, Valerie.
Title: Weather / Valerie Harvey.
Description: Buffalo, NY : KidHaven Publishing, 2027. | Series: Super science | Includes glossary and index.
Identifiers: ISBN 9781534570405 (pbk.) | ISBN 9781534570412 (library bound) | ISBN 9781534570429 (ebook)
Subjects: LCSH: Weather--Juvenile literature.
Classification: LCC QC981.3 H378 2027 | DDC 551.6--dc23

Printed in China

CPSIA compliance information: Batch #QS27KH: For further information contact Greenhaven Publishing LLC at 1-844-317-7404.

Please visit our website, www.greenhavenpublishing.com. For a free color catalog of all our high-quality books, call toll free 1-844-317-7404 or fax 1-844-317-7405.

Find us on

Image Credits. All images courtesy of Shutterstock.com, unless otherwise stated.
Cover – FamVeld, Leremy. Recurring – Leremy, Dedraw Studio. 4–5 – Kinwunz, Leremy. 6–7 – Kittyfly, Stella_E. 8–9 – Alexlukin, GBJSTOCK. 10–11 – Mr.Prasit BOONMA, hecke61. 12–13 – Quality Stock Arts, FamVeld. 14–15 – Iryna Inshyna, Creative Travel Projects. 16–17 – Just dance, Olga_Kuzmina. 18–19 – Denis Torkhov, Hasantha Lakmal, savitskaya iryna. 20–21 – Traveller70, Ronnysteve. 22–23 – Graphic421.

CONTENTS

Words that look like this can be found in the glossary on page 24.

SUPER START!

When we ask questions, make predictions, and test ideas, we call it science. Science helps us figure out how the world works. Scientists use experiments to find out what things are made of and why they do what they do.

Captain Curious loves science that happens in the sky. He'll be our helper as we discover how weather forms, why it changes and what clues the sky gives us about what's coming next.

WONDERFUL WEATHER

Weather is all around us every single day! It changes the sky, the air, and even how we feel. Weather is like Earth's way of showing off its superpowers.

Some days weather warms us, some days it cools us, and some days it surprises us! This might seem like magic, but it's actually science! Let's explore the different types of weather.

SUNSHINE

Sunshine is Earth's bright and cheerful superpower. The sun gives off light and heat. That light and heat travels to us through space. It keeps our planet warm and helps plants grow.

Sunshine helps our bodies stay healthy and can even help us to feel happy. The sun is our giant glowing hero in the sky!

Too much sunshine can be harmful. Always wear sunscreen outside!

CLOUDS

Clouds can be big and fluffy or thin and wispy. They are made when tiny drops of water in the sky come together. All clouds have an amazing superpower—they can change their shape!

Some clouds look soft like pillows. Others grow big and dark when they are ready to rain. Clouds help to control Earth's temperature. They can trap heat as well as bounce sunlight back into space.

RAIN

Rain is Earth's refreshing superpower. It falls from clouds when water droplets join together and get too heavy. Rain fills rivers and lakes, helps to water plants, and keeps animals hydrated.

Clouds, rain, rivers, lakes, oceans, and even puddles are all part of the water cycle. All water gets recycled as it moves around our planet.

SNOW AND ICE

Snow and ice are Earth's chilly superpowers. Snowflakes form when tiny drops of water freeze into beautiful crystal shapes. Each snowflake is unique. Snowflakes fall from clouds to make snow.

When water is very cold, it freezes and turns into frost and ice. Frost and ice can cover ponds, rooftops, and trees. They make the world look like it's sparkling!

WIND

Wind is Earth's whooshing, rushing superpower of moving air. It's created when warm air rises and cool air slides in to take its place.

Wind can be gentle like a whisper or strong like a speedy superhero. It helps plants spread their seeds, moves clouds across the sky, and even turns wind turbines to make electricity.

STORMS

Storms are some of the most powerful types of weather. They happen when warm and cool air bump into each other. Thunder rumbles, lightning flashes, and rain pours.

Storms can shake up the sky!

When electricity builds up inside storm clouds, it gets released as lightning. Every flash of lightning is a huge spark of electricity.

CLIMATES

Climates are what the weather of a place is like over a long time. Some places stay warm and sunny, and other places are cold and snowy. Some places switch between different seasons.

From wet rainforests to dry deserts to icy poles, each climate has its own weather superpowers. Different plants and animals live and grow in each climate.

SUPER SCIENCE CHALLENGE

Are you ready to become a science superhero? Take this quiz and check your answers on page 23.

1. The sun helps plants grow by giving them light and warmth. (True/False)

2. Clouds are made of fluffy cotton that floats in the sky. (True/False)

3. Rain happens when water droplets in clouds get too heavy and fall. (True/False)

4. Snowflakes are all exactly the same shape. (True/False)

5. Wind is moving air that can be gentle or strong. (True/False)

You have completed this Super Science book and have now become a

★ SCIENCE SUPERHERO! ★

Keep exploring, asking questions, and discovering amazing things about the world.

Answers:
1. True. 2. False: Clouds are made of tiny water droplets. 3. True. 4. False: Every snowflake is unique. 5. True.

GLOSSARY

EXPERIMENTS	tests to work things out and find out new things about something
FREEZE	when water hardens into ice
HYDRATED	having enough water in the body
PREDICTIONS	guesses about things that could happen based on evidence and facts
RECYCLED	used again to make something else
SEASONS	different parts of the year based on changes in the weather
TEMPERATURE	how hot or cold something is
UNIQUE	unlike anything else

INDEX